# Introduction

Horses have a way of capturing our [hearts]. Whether it's their gentle eyes, pow[erful presence, or the] freedom they inspire, horses hold a [special place in the hearts of] many. For those who dream of riding, [caring for, or simply learn]ing about these magnificent creatures, this book is the perfect guide to get started.

In **"The Ultimate Horse and Pony Handbook"**, you'll discover the fascinating world of horses, from their unique behaviors and incredible abilities to the joys of riding and caring for them. This book is designed to inspire young horse enthusiasts and give them the knowledge they need to dive into the world of equestrian adventure. Whether you've already met your favorite pony or are just beginning your journey, this book will help you build a strong foundation.

## About the Author

Diane Vervaet has been passionate about horses for as long as she can remember. Her journey began at age 14 when she got her first horse, a dream come true for a young girl who spent countless hours imagining life in the saddle. Later, as a young adult, she welcomed a beautiful purebred Arabian colt into her life. Diane trained him herself, teaching him to ride, navigate trails, perform low jumps, and they even learned to pull a cart. This special bond sparked a lifelong dedication to horses.

As Diane's love for horses grew, so did her involvement in the equestrian world. She started and ran a thriving boarding and lesson stable, where she worked with riders of all ages and skill levels. From beginners just starting their equestrian journey to students pursuing competitive goals, Diane's lesson horses were carefully chosen to provide safe and joyful learning experiences. At the same time, she worked with instructors and coaches on her own skills and experiences including side-saddle, cross country jumping, and saddle seat and earned her medal in vaulting.

Throughout her life, Diane loved riding in various equestrian disciplines, including hunters, dressage and Western riding. Her dedication and skill took her to higher-level dressage competitions with some of her most beloved horses.

Diane has three children who have all learned to ride and love horses and animals. Over the years there have always been lots of animals that we include in our life and consider to be part of the family. Diane hopes to always have horses and pets in her life. Through this book, she shares her wealth of experience and enthusiasm to inspire a new generation of horse lovers.

**Let's saddle up and begin an unforgettable adventure into the world of horses and ponies!**

# Horses and Ponies

Please help us continue to bring joy to others by leaving a review!

Thank you for your purchase!

**Twigg Publishing**
See all of our books to purchase or leave a review. Simply scan this QR code.

Copyright © [2025] by [Twigg Publishing]

All rights reserved.
No portion of this book may be reproduced, distributed or transmitted in any form without written permission from the publisher or author, except as permitted by U.S. copyright law.

# The Ultimate Horse and Pony Handbook:

A Young Horse Lover's Guide to Horses, Ponies, and Riding Fun

DIANE VERVAET

TWIGG PUBLISHING

*For all the horses I was lucky enough
to have in my life, especially
Cayenne, Zorba and Boerne,
who taught me the most!*

# Table of Contents

**Chapter 1:**
Why We Love Horses .......... 1

**Chapter 2:**
From Stable to Service: Horses and Ponies at Work .......... 4

**Chapter 3:**
Fun Facts About Horses and Ponies to Amaze You! .......... 18

**Chapter 4:**
Horse Talk: Learning the Language of Riding .......... 23

**Chapter 5:**
Breeds of Horses and Ponies .......... 29

**Chapter 6:**
Most Common Riding Styles and Saddles .......... 43

**Chapter 7:**
Taking Care of a Horse or Pony .......... 49

**Chapter 8:**
Getting Ready for Riding Lessons .......... 56

**Chapter 9:**
Tacking Up Your Horse or Pony .......... 60

**Chapter 10:**
Let's Begin Riding! .......... 66

**Chapter 11:**
Continue Your Riding Adventures .......... 71

CHAPTER 1

# Why We Love Horses

Horses are some of the most extraordinary animals in the world. They capture our hearts with their beauty, strength, and gentle spirits. People of all ages are drawn to horses for many reasons, and kids often find them to be magical companions. But what is it about horses that makes them so lovable? Let's explore!

## Sweet and Sensitive Souls

One of the most remarkable things about horses is their sweet and sensitive nature. Horses have an incredible ability to understand and respond to human emotions. When you're happy, they seem to share your joy. If you're feeling sad, a horse might nuzzle you gently, offering quiet comfort. This sensitivity makes horses wonderful friends and loyal companions.

Horses are also very intelligent animals. They can sense your mood and often act in ways that show they care. When you spend time with a horse, you'll notice how closely they pay attention to you. Whether it's the way they flick their ears to listen or look at you with their big, kind eyes, horses have a special way of making you feel understood.

## Soft and Beautiful

Have you ever run your hand over a horse's coat? It's one of the most soothing things in the world. A horse's coat is soft and smooth, like velvet under your fingertips. Their manes and tails are often thick and silky, making it fun to braid or brush them. Grooming a horse isn't just about keeping them clean; it's also a wonderful way to bond.

And let's not forget how amazing horses smell! Many horse lovers talk about the unique, earthy scent of a horse—a mix of sunshine, hay, and warm fur. It's a comforting smell that brings a sense of calm and happiness. Spending time around horses isn't just fun; it feels good for your heart and soul.

## Big, Gentle Giants

Despite their size, horses are some of the gentlest creatures you'll ever meet. They're careful around people, especially kids, and seem to understand the importance of being gentle. When you stand next to a horse, it's easy to feel a mix of awe and admiration. Their strength and grace are inspiring, but their kindness is what truly makes them lovable.

Horses love to form connections with humans. They enjoy being petted, brushed, and spoken to softly. Spending time with a horse can feel like having a conversation without words. They'll greet you with a soft whinny, nuzzle your hand, or follow you around the pasture, showing their affection in their own unique way.

## A Bond Like No Other

The bond between humans and horses is truly special. Horses have been our companions for thousands of years, helping us work, travel, and explore. But more than that, they've been our friends. Riding a horse or simply being near one creates a sense of connection that's hard to put into words. It's a feeling of trust and partnership that grows stronger the more time you spend together.

So, why do we love horses? Because they love us back. They teach us patience, kindness, and the joy of living in the moment. Horses remind us to appreciate the beauty of nature and the power of friendship. Whether you dream of riding across open fields or simply enjoying a quiet moment in their company, horses have a way of making life feel a little more magical.

CHAPTER 2

# From Stable to Service: Horses and Ponies at Work

Horses and ponies aren't just lovable, they're also incredibly versatile! They can do so many amazing things and have jobs that help people in all kinds of ways. Let's take a look and learn about the interesting roles horses and ponies play.

## Show Horses: Stars of the Equestrian World

Show horses are the athletes of the equestrian world, dazzling audiences with their skills, beauty, and precision. Whether soaring over fences, performing intricate dance-like movements, or showing off their smooth gaits, show horses compete in a wide variety of disciplines. Each discipline highlights the unique abilities and talents of these incredible animals, as well as the deep partnership between horse and rider.

### Jumping: Soaring Over Obstacles

In show jumping, horses and riders navigate a series of fences, walls, and other obstacles, aiming to clear them cleanly without knocking anything down. Speed and precision are key in this excit-

ing discipline, as competitors race against the clock to finish with the fastest time and fewest faults.

Jumping courses can include a variety of challenges, such as combinations of fences placed close together, requiring the horse to adjust their stride. Horses used for jumping are often bold, athletic, and quick thinkers, with breeds like Thoroughbreds and Warmbloods excelling in this high-energy sport.

Watching a horse gracefully leap over a towering jump is thrilling and a true testament to their athleticism and trust in their rider.

## Dressage: The Art of Precision

Dressage is often described as "horse ballet" because it focuses on the harmony and communication between horse and rider. In dressage, horses perform a series of carefully choreographed movements, such as pirouettes, flying lead changes, and lateral movements. The goal is to make these complex maneuvers look effortless and natural, as though the horse is performing on their own.

Dressage competitors are judged on their accuracy, elegance, and how smoothly the horse and rider work together. Some advanced routines are even set to music, creating a breathtaking performance. Breeds like Warmbloods, Andalusians, and Friesians often excel in this discipline due to their strength and graceful movement.

Dressage showcases the incredible bond and trust that develop between horse and rider through years of training.

## Western Riding: Style and Versatility

Western riding competitions celebrate the skills developed on ranches and trails. These events are steeped in tradition, with riders often wearing cowboy hats, boots, and Western-style outfits. Some popular Western riding disciplines include:

**Western Pleasure:** Horses are judged on their smooth gaits and relaxed demeanor. Riders guide their horses through slow, steady movements, showing their responsiveness and calm attitude.

**Reining:** Often called "Western dressage," reining tests a horse's

ability to perform precise patterns, including spins, sliding stops, and lead changes.

**Barrel Racing:** A high-speed event where riders guide their horses around a cloverleaf pattern of barrels. Speed, agility, and tight turns are essential to winning.

**Trail Classes:** Horses navigate obstacles like gates, bridges, and poles, demonstrating their calmness and problem-solving skills.

Breeds like Quarter Horses, Appaloosas, and Paint Horses are common in Western disciplines. They are prized for their versatility, steady temperament, and athletic build.

## The Dedication of Show Horses

Competing in any discipline requires years of training, a strong partnership between horse and rider, and a commitment to excellence. Show horses must be physically fit, mentally sharp, and willing to perform under pressure. Their riders and trainers work tirelessly to refine their skills, preparing for competitions that test their abilities to the fullest.

### The Magic of Show Horses

Show horses bring excitement, elegance, and inspiration to audiences around the world. Whether you're watching a horse soar over a jump, perform a perfect pirouette, or smoothly navigate a trail course, it's clear that these animals are more than just competitors—they're stars.

Each discipline celebrates the unique talents of these extraordinary animals, showcasing the beauty, power, and grace that make horses so special. For those lucky enough to compete with or watch show horses, the experience is unforgettable.

## Parade Horses: Showstoppers on the Streets

Horses have a special way of turning any event into something magical, and parade horses are no exception. These horses are trained to march proudly through city streets or along festival routes, often accompanied by music, cheering crowds, and vibrant decorations. Their calm demeanor, dazzling appearances, and ability to stay focused make them perfect for creating unforgettable spectacles.

## The Role of Parade Horses

Parade horses are responsible for adding elegance, tradition, and excitement to parades. From Fourth of July celebrations to state fairs and holiday events, they bring charm and grandeur to any occasion. Many parade horses are decorated with ribbons, bells, or flowers, and they often pull beautifully adorned carriages or wagons. The bond between parade horses and their handlers is crucial—they work together to navigate the lively atmosphere with grace and precision.

## The Budweiser Clydesdales: Parade Royalty

One of the most famous groups of parade horses in the world is the Budweiser Clydesdales. These majestic, gentle giants are known for their towering size, flowing white feathering around their hooves, and perfectly matched teams. Each horse stands about 18 hands high (6 feet at the shoulders) and weighs up to 2,000 pounds, making them true showstoppers.

The Budweiser Clydesdales have been delighting parade audiences for nearly a century. They travel in specially designed trailers,

and their handlers take great care to ensure they look their best for every appearance. The horses pull a gleaming red beer wagon and are often accompanied by a Dalmatian, who rides on the wagon as a nod to historical traditions.

These horses have become icons of American culture, representing hard work, teamwork, and celebration. Watching the Budweiser Clydesdales march in a parade is a sight to remember, and their appearances are always a highlight of any event.

## Police Horses: Guardians of the Parade

Another equally impressive sight in the parade is the mounted police unit. Police horses are not only beautiful—they're also highly trained and play an important role in ensuring public safety. These horses must remain calm in noisy, crowded environments and respond instantly to their rider's commands.

During parades, police horses help control the flow of spectators, clear paths for floats and performers, and maintain order. Their size and presence command respect, and they are often admired for their elegance and professionalism. Watching a police horse in action reminds us of their versatility and the special bond they share with their riders.

**Training Parade Horses**

Not every horse can handle the hustle and bustle of a parade. Parade horses go through special training, similar to the training for a Police horse, to help them stay calm around large crowds, loud noises, and unfamiliar environments. They practice walking in step with other horses, ignoring distractions, and responding to their handler's cues.

Horses chosen for parades must have a calm temperament, good health, and the ability to maintain their composure under pressure. Their training often includes exposure to music, horns, and other sounds to prepare them for the big day.

## Ranch Horses: The Hard-Working Heroes of the Range

Ranch horses are the unsung heroes of the Western world. These versatile and hardworking horses are the backbone of daily life on cattle ranches, performing essential tasks that require strength, intelligence, and stamina. Whether they're herding cattle, navigating rough terrain, or lending a helping hoof in the branding pen, ranch horses are true partners to the cowboys and ranchers who rely on them.

**The Role of Ranch Horses**

Life on a ranch is tough, and a good ranch horse needs to be tougher. Their primary job is to help with cattle work, which includes herding, cutting, and sorting livestock. A skilled ranch horse can anticipate a cow's movements, respond to subtle cues from their rider, and maneuver quickly to keep the herd in check.

But their responsibilities don't stop there. Ranch horses are also used for:

**Checking fences:** They help ranchers cover large areas of land to inspect and repair fences.

**Roping:** In the branding pen or out on the range, ranch horses help hold cattle steady during vaccinations or branding.

**Trail riding:** Ranch horses carry their riders across miles of rugged terrain, often climbing hills, crossing rivers, and handling unpredictable conditions.

Ranch horses must be calm, reliable, and ready to work long hours. Their ability to stay focused and handle unexpected challenges makes them indispensable.

**Characteristics of a Good Ranch Horse**

Ranch horses come in all shapes and sizes, but certain traits make them particularly well-suited for the job:

**Stamina:** Ranch work requires hours of physical effort, so these horses need endurance to keep going all day.

**Agility:** Whether they're weaving through a herd or chasing a stray cow, ranch horses must be quick on their feet and highly maneuverable.

**Intelligence:** Ranch horses are problem-solvers. They learn to think independently and respond to subtle commands.

**Calm Temperament:** A good ranch horse stays steady and quiet, even in chaotic situations like moving a large herd or handling a stubborn cow.

Breeds like Quarter Horses, known for their quick reflexes and sturdy builds, dominate the ranching world. Other popular breeds include Appaloosas, Paint Horses, and even certain hardy Mustang types.

## Training a Ranch Horse

Ranch horses undergo extensive training to prepare them for the demands of their work. They learn to respond to the rider's cues, such as subtle shifts in weight or light touches on the reins. Many are also trained in "cow sense," the ability to read and predict a cow's movements—an essential skill for herding and cutting. Ranch horses are taught to work individually and as part of a team. Whether they're separating a single cow from the herd or joining a group to drive cattle across open fields, their training ensures they can handle a variety of tasks with confidence.

## The Versatility of Ranch Horses

One of the most remarkable things about ranch horses is their versatility. Many of them excel in other equestrian disciplines, including rodeo events like team roping and barrel racing. Their experience on the ranch gives them the agility, responsiveness, and calm demeanor needed to shine in the arena.

## The Bond Between Rancher and Horse

Ranch horses aren't just tools—they're trusted partners. The bond between a rancher and their horse runs deep, built on mutual respect and countless hours spent working together. A ranch horse often knows their rider's habits and preferences, and the rider knows their horse's quirks and strengths.

This partnership is what makes ranch horses so special. They aren't just helping hands—they're part of the ranching family.

## The Heart of the Ranch

Ranch horses are the heart and soul of life on the range. Their strength, intelligence, and dedication make them invaluable, and their quiet heroism keeps the ranch running smoothly. Whether they're driving cattle across open plains or standing patiently in the branding pen, ranch horses are a testament to the incredible partnership between humans and horses. They are truly the hardworking heroes of the Western world.

# Therapy Horses, Guide Ponies, and Support Ponies: Gentle Helpers Changing Lives

Horses and ponies are more than just companions or athletes; they're also healers and helpers. Their calm, sensitive nature and ability to connect with people make them ideal partners for individuals with physical, emotional, or developmental challenges. Therapy horses, guide ponies, and assist-and-support ponies play vital roles in improving lives, offering support, comfort, and independence to those who need it most.

## Therapy Horses: Healing Through Connection

Therapy horses are at the heart of equine-assisted therapy programs, which help people of all ages facing a variety of challenges. These horses work with individuals who have physical disabilities, emotional trauma, or developmental conditions like autism.

In equine-assisted therapy, participants interact with horses in activities such as grooming, leading, or riding. These experiences promote physical, emotional, and social growth in a way that feels more like play than therapy. For example:

**Physical Therapy:** Riding a horse mimics the motion of walking, helping individuals improve balance, coordination, and muscle strength.

**Emotional Healing:** Spending time with a gentle, nonjudgmental therapy horse can reduce anxiety, build confidence, and provide a sense of calm.

**Social Skills:** Interacting with therapy horses teaches patience, communication, and responsibility.

Horses chosen for therapy programs are calm, patient, and responsive to the needs of the individuals they work with. Breeds like Quarter Horses, Haflingers, and Fjord Ponies are popular choices because of their steady temperaments and manageable sizes.

## Guide Ponies: Navigating the World

Did you know that some ponies are trained to serve as guide animals, just like guide dogs? Guide ponies help people with visual impairments navigate their surroundings safely. Their small size, long lifespan, and calm demeanor make them a great alternative to dogs for individuals who may have allergies or prefer equines.

Guide ponies are trained to:
- Lead their handlers around obstacles
- Signal when there are changes in elevation, like stairs or curbs
- Stop and wait for their handler's next command

These ponies wear special harnesses and work closely with their handlers to ensure their safety. Their loyalty and intelligence make them exceptional companions, and their service provides individuals with greater independence and mobility.

## Assist and Support Ponies: Lending a Helping Hoof

Assist and support ponies are specially trained to help individuals with physical or emotional challenges in their daily lives. These ponies are not just helpers—they're also companions, providing comfort and emotional support.

Some tasks assist-and-support ponies may perform include:
- Opening and closing doors
- Retrieving dropped items
- Providing stability for individuals with mobility challenges
- Offering emotional reassurance during stressful situations

Their patient and intuitive nature makes them ideal for individuals who benefit from a constant, calming presence. Shetland Ponies and Miniature Horses are commonly used because of their manageable size, adaptability, and gentle personalities.

## The Impact of These Special Horses and Ponies

Therapy horses, guide ponies, and assist-and-support ponies touch lives in profound ways. They bring hope and healing, foster independence, and provide a unique kind of companionship that only an animal as empathetic as a horse or pony can offer.

Their work reminds us of the incredible bond between humans and equines, showing just how much these gentle creatures can enrich our lives. Whether they're helping someone walk confidently down the street or offering a moment of peace during a difficult time, these special horses and ponies are true heroes in their own right.

CHAPTER 3
# Fun Facts About Horses and Ponies to Amaze You!

Horses and ponies are amazing animals with some pretty cool tricks up their sleeves. Here are some fun and surprising facts that will make you say, "Wow!"

### 1. Horses Can Sleep Standing Up

Horses have a special ability to sleep while standing! They lock their leg joints so they don't fall over. But they do lie down for a deep sleep every now and then.

### 2. Horses Have Incredible Memories

Horses never forget a face! They can remember people and other horses for years. If you've ever been kind to a horse, chances are they'll remember you the next time they see you.

### 3. Ponies Are Super Strong

Don't let their small size fool you—ponies are incredibly strong for their size! They can carry heavy loads and pull carts with ease. In fact, pound for pound, ponies are often stronger than horses!

## 4. Horses Have Huge Eyes

Horses have the largest eyes of any land mammal! Their eyes are on the sides of their heads, which gives them almost 360-degree vision. This helps them spot danger no matter where it's coming from.

## 5. Horses Can't Throw Up

Unlike humans, horses can't vomit. That's why it's so important for them to eat the right food and chew it thoroughly!

## 6. They Communicate with Their Ears

Horses use their ears to "talk." They swivel them around to show what they're paying attention to, and if their ears are pinned back, it means they're upset. Pay attention to their ears, and you'll know how they're feeling!

## 7. Horses Can Run Soon After Birth

A foal (a baby horse) can stand, walk, and even run just hours after being born. They need to keep up with their moms to stay safe in the wild.

## 8. Horses Have Amazing Speeds

The fastest recorded gallop of a horse was about 55 miles per hour! That's as fast as a car on the highway. Most horses, though, gallop at around 25–30 miles per hour.

## 9. Ponies Live a Long Time

Ponies often live longer than horses, with some living into their 30s or even 40s. That's a lot of time to make memories with their humans!

## 10. Horses Can Make Funny Faces

Have you ever seen a horse curl their upper lip and make a goofy face? That's called the flehmen response. They're using it to smell better and figure out what's around them!

## 11. Horses Have More Bones Than You

Horses have 205 bones in their bodies—one more than humans. Most of these are in their legs, which makes them strong and flexible.

## 12. Horses and Ponies Have Best Friends

Horses and ponies are social animals and often form close friendships with other horses in their herd. They even get sad when they're separated from their best buddy!

## 13. They Can Drink a LOT of Water

A horse can drink up to 10 gallons of water a day! That's about as much as 160 cups of water. On hot days or after lots of exercise, they might drink even more.

## 14. They Can Laugh

Okay, they're not really laughing, but when horses curl their lips up and show their teeth, it looks like they're cracking up! They're actually trying to pick up scents in the air.

## 15. Horses Have Special Feet

A horse's hoof is made of keratin, the same stuff that makes up your hair and fingernails. They need regular trimming and care to keep them healthy, just like you need to clip your nails!

## 16. Horse or Pony

Any horse that measures 14.3 hands or less at the withers is considered a pony.

## 17. Horses Have Really Fast Hair Growth

A horse's mane and tail grow faster than most humans' hair—sometimes as much as 1 inch per month!

## 18. Horses have amazing vision!

They can see almost 360 degrees around them, but they can't see directly in front of or behind themselves.

## 19. Their Whiskers Help Them "See" Up Close

Horses use their whiskers around their nose to feel objects because their eyes can't focus on things right in front of them.

## 20. Some horses have unique mustaches!

Certain breeds, like the Gypsy Vanner, can grow adorable mustaches.

## 21. Horses have super strong teeth!

Their teeth take up more space in their head than their brain does!

## 22. Ponies are geniuses at puzzles!

Ponies are known for being clever and can figure out how to open gates or untie knots.

## 23. Horses can hear better than humans!

Their ears can swivel 180 degrees to pick up sounds from all around.

## 24. Horses have a special handshake!

They greet each other by blowing air through their noses to exchange scents, like a friendly sniff.

## 25. A group of horses is called a "herd."

In the wild, herds are led by a bossy female horse called a "lead mare."

Horses and ponies are full of surprises. The more you get to know them, the more you'll discover just how amazing they really are!

CHAPTER 4

# Horse Talk: Learning the Language of Riding

When you start horseback riding, one of the first things you'll notice is that there's a whole new language to learn. From understanding the horse's movements to following your instructor's directions, "horse talk" is essential for every rider. Knowing the correct terms makes riding safer, easier, and more enjoyable—and it helps you communicate clearly with both your horse and your instructor.

## Basic Horse Gaits and Commands

Horses move in different patterns called **gaits**, and each gait has its own rhythm and speed. Here are the main ones every rider should know:

**Walk:** The slowest gait, where the horse moves one foot at a time in a steady, four-beat rhythm.

**Trot:** A two-beat gait that's faster than a walk. You'll feel the horse bounce as their diagonal legs move together.

**Canter:** A three-beat gait that's smooth and faster than a trot but

slower than a gallop. It is also called a Lope in Western terms.

**Gallop:** The fastest gait, where the horse moves in a four-beat pattern at high speed.

To guide your horse, you'll use simple commands that your instructor will teach you:

**"Walk on":** This tells the horse to start walking.

**"Whoa":** A command to stop.

**"Trot" or "Canter":** These signal the horse to move into the next gait.

**"Back":** A cue to ask the horse to step backward.

## Horse Talk Around the Riding Stable

Continuing to learn the language of horseback riding will help you communicate even better with your instructor and understand what's happening around the stable. Here are a few more common terms to know:

**Halter:** Goes on the head of the horse like a **Bridle** but without a **Bit**. It is used with a Lead line to lead the horse.

**Tack:** All the equipment used for riding, including the saddle, bridle, and saddle pad.

**Tack up:** This means getting the horse ready to ride. It usually refers to putting on the saddle and bridle after the horse is groomed.

**Saddle Pad:** The pad or blanket that cushions the **Saddle** on the horse. It also absorbs sweat from the horse to keep the saddle cleaner.

**Girth:** Used to secure the saddle on the horse.

**Stirrups:** Your feet go here, and they are attached to the saddle with the **Stirrup Leathers**.

**Reins:** The straps on the bridle that are connected to the bit in the horse's mouth that you hold gently to guide the horse.

**Mount:** To get on the horse.

**Mounting Block:** It resembles small, sturdy steps with a flat top for standing on while mounting your horse.

**Dismount:** To get off the horse. Never use the mounting block to dismount. Always dismount directly onto the ground for safety purposes.

**Stall:** The individual place in the barn where each horse lives.

**Mucking out:** The term used to clean the horse's stall.

**Paddock:** Usually a small fenced-in area or pasture designed for one or two horses to go outside for some fresh air and exercise. Some horses prefer to be in a paddock rather than a stall.

**Hands:** A unit of measurement for a horse's height, equal to 4 inches. A horse that is 14.2 hands tall is 58 inches at the withers.

**Near Side:** The horse's left side is traditionally used for mounting and dismounting.

**Off Side:** The right side of the horse.

**Halt:** An instructor's command to you to stop your horse.

**Half Seat:** A riding position where the rider's seat is slightly out of the saddle, often used for jumping or faster gaits. It is also sometimes called the **Jump Seat**.

**Post:** Rising out of the saddle in rhythm with the horse's trot to make the ride smoother.

**Ground Rails:** Poles are laid flat on the ground so the horse can step over during training or practice.

**On the Bit:** A term that means the horse is working correctly, with their head and neck in a rounded position, responding to the rider's aids.

Don't worry if you don't remember everything right away—your instructor will guide you as you learn!

## Why Equestrian Vocabulary Matters

Learning horse talk isn't just about sounding like a rider—it's about understanding your instructor, communicating effectively with your horse, and building confidence. Here's why it's so important:

**Clear Communication:** Knowing the correct terms helps you follow your instructor's directions during lessons. For example, if they say, "Use your half seat over the ground rails," you'll know what to do.

**Confidence Booster:** Familiarity with riding vocabulary helps you feel more comfortable and capable around horses, especially in a lesson or group setting.

**Better Connection with Your Horse:** Using clear commands helps your horse understand what you're asking, creating a stronger partnership.

## Practicing Horse Talk

The best way to learn horse talk is to practice! Here are some fun ways to reinforce your new vocabulary:

**Use Activity books for games and puzzles:** Activity books with various word puzzles are a great and fun way for learning and remembering horse vocabulary.

**Play Vocabulary Games:** Create a matching game with flashcards that pair terms with pictures of tack, gaits, or horse body parts.

**Flashcards for Memorization:** Write terms on one side of a card and definitions or drawings on the other. Quiz yourself or a friend.

**Use the Words in Real Life:** Practice saying commands like "Walk on" or "Whoa" during lessons and point out tack parts as you groom or saddle your horse.

**Join Discussions:** Talk with your instructor or friends about what you're learning. The more you use the terms, the easier they'll stick.

## The Power of Horse Talk

Learning the language of riding is a vital part of becoming a skilled and confident equestrian. As you become familiar with these terms, you'll find it easier to follow instructions, communicate with your horse, and feel like a true rider. Before you know it, you'll be speaking horse talk like a pro!

CHAPTER 5
# Breeds of Horses and Ponies

Horses and ponies come in a variety of breeds, each with unique characteristics that make them special. Some breeds are well known worldwide, while others are rare and less commonly seen. Did you know that any horse under 14.3 hands high is considered a pony? Let's dive into the fascinating world of horse and pony breeds.

# Common Horse Breeds

## Thoroughbred

**Origin:** England

**Characteristics:** Thoroughbreds are bred for speed and endurance, primarily for horse racing. They are tall and elegant with a lean, muscular body, long neck, and long legs. Known for their spirited and energetic temperament, they require experienced handling.

**Size:** Typically stand between 15.2 to 17 hands (62 to 68 inches) at the shoulder.

**Uses:** Racing is their primary focus, but they also excel in jumping, eventing, fox hunting, and dressage.

## Quarter Horse

**Origin:** United States

**Characteristics:** The Quarter Horse is named for its ability to sprint faster than any other horse over short distances (a quarter mile or less). They have a stocky, muscular build with powerful hindquarters and a calm, cooperative temperament.

**Size:** Stand between 14.3 to 16 hands (59 to 64 inches).

**Uses:** Widely used in Western disciplines like barrel racing, reining, and cutting, as well as ranch work, trail riding, and rodeo events. Their versatility makes them one of the most popular horse breeds.

## Arabian

**Origin:** Middle East

**Characteristics:** Arabians are one of the oldest and most recognizable horse breeds, prized for their beauty, endurance, and intelligence. They have a distinctive dished face, large expressive eyes, arched neck, and a high-set tail. They bond strongly with humans and are known for their friendly and curious temperament.

**Size:** Generally smaller, standing between 14.1 to 15.1 hands (57 to 61 inches).

**Uses:** Famous for endurance riding, Arabians are also used in dressage, pleasure riding, and as family horses.

## Warmblood

**Origin:** Europe (Germany, Netherlands, and other countries)

**Characteristics:** Warmbloods are a group of sport horse breeds (e.g., Dutch Warmblood, Hanoverian, Oldenburg) bred for competition. They have an athletic build, with a balanced frame, strong legs, and fluid movement. They are known for their excellent temperament—calm yet responsive.

**Size:** Stand between 15.2 to 17.2 hands (62 to 68 inches).

**Uses:** Primarily bred for equestrian sports such as dressage, show jumping, and eventing. Their versatility also makes them popular in riding schools and competitions.

## Clydesdale

**Origin:** Scotland

**Characteristics:** These gentle giants are draft horses known for their incredible strength, size, and feathered legs. They have a broad chest, powerful shoulders, and a calm, friendly personality, making them easy to work with despite their size.

**Size:** Stand between 16 to 18 hands (64 to 72 inches) and weigh over 2,000 pounds in some cases.

**Uses:** Traditionally used for heavy pulling in agriculture and transportation, today they are seen in carriage driving, promotional events (e.g., Budweiser Clydesdales), and parades.

## Paint Horse

**Origin:** United States

**Characteristics:** Paint Horses are known for their striking, colorful coat patterns (e.g., overo, tobiano, and tovero). They share many physical traits with Quarter Horses, including a muscular build and powerful hindquarters. They are friendly, versatile, and intelligent, making them ideal for riders of all levels.

**Size:** Stand between 14.2 to 16 hands (58 to 64 inches).

**Uses:** Popular in Western riding disciplines like trail riding, reining, and barrel racing. Their unique coats also make them favorites for parades and showmanship events.

## Appaloosa

**Origin:** North America (developed by the Nez Perce Native American tribe)

**Characteristics:** The Appaloosa is famous for its colorful spotted coat, which comes in patterns like leopard, blanket, snowflake, and more. They have unique physical traits, including mottled skin (especially on the muzzle), striped hooves, and a white sclera around their eyes. Appaloosas are known for their intelligence, versatility, and friendly demeanor, forming strong bonds with their handlers.

**Size:** Typically stand between 14.2 to 16 hands (58 to 64 inches).

**Uses:** Appaloosas excel in various disciplines, including trail riding, Western events like barrel racing and reining, endurance riding, and even English events such as jumping and dressage. Their sure-footedness makes them exceptional companions for riders exploring rough or challenging terrain.

## Friesian Horse

**Origin:** Netherlands (Friesland region)

**Characteristics:** The Friesian horse is known for its stunning black coat, flowing mane and tail, and graceful movement. They have a powerful, well-muscled build with an arched neck, expressive head, and feathering on their lower legs. Friesians are famous for their elegant, high-stepping trot and their gentle, willing temperament, making them a favorite in both classical

and modern equestrian disciplines.

**Size:** Typically stand between 15 to 17 hands (60 to 68 inches) at the withers.

**Uses:** Friesians excel in dressage, carriage driving, and exhibitions due to their impressive appearance and movement. They are also used for pleasure riding and in films and reenactments because of their majestic presence and trainability.

## Percheron Horse

**Origin:** France (Perche region)

**Characteristics:** The Percheron is a powerful and versatile draft horse known for its strength, intelligence, and elegant appearance. They have a muscular, well-proportioned build with a broad chest, strong legs, and a refined head. Unlike some draft breeds, Percherons can have a more refined and graceful movement, often exhibiting a smooth and energetic trot. Their coats are commonly black or gray, though other colors can occur. Despite their size, they are gentle and willing, making them excellent working and companion animals.

**Size:** Typically stand between 15.2 to 19 hands (62 to 76 inches) at the withers and can weigh between 1,800 to 2,600 pounds.

**Uses:** Traditionally used for heavy farm work, carriage driving, and hauling, Percherons are now popular in logging, parades, and competitive driving events. They are also used for riding, particularly in dressage and pleasure riding due to their smooth gaits and trainability.

## Miniature Horse (Not a Pony!)

**Origin:** Europe (developed from small horse breeds over centuries)

**Characteristics:** Miniature horses are known for their small stature while retaining the refined proportions of full-sized horses.

They have a well-balanced body, expressive eyes, and a variety of coat colors and patterns. Despite their size, they are strong, intelligent, and gentle, often forming close bonds with their owners.

**Size:** Stand under 34 to 38 inches (8.5 to 9.5 hands) at the withers, depending on breed registry standards.

**Uses:** Miniature horses are popular as therapy animals, companion pets, and in competitive driving events. They are also used in educational programs and even as service animals for individuals with disabilities.

## Common Pony Breeds

### Shetland Pony

**Origin:** Shetland Islands, Scotland

**Characteristics:** Shetland ponies are one of the smallest but strongest pony breeds, often described as "tiny powerhouses." They have a thick double coat to withstand harsh climates, a sturdy build, short legs, and a dense mane and tail. They are intelligent,

hardy, and often a little cheeky, making them fun but sometimes stubborn companions.

**Size:** Stand under 11 hands (44 inches) at the withers.

**Uses:** Popular for children's riding, driving carts, and as companions. Historically used in coal mines due to their strength and small size.

## Welsh Pony

**Origin:** Wales

**Characteristics:** Welsh ponies come in four sections (A, B, C, D), varying by size and type, but all share the breed's elegance, intelligence, and versatility. They are hardy, sure-footed, and have a beautiful, refined appearance with a dished face and flowing mane and tail. Welsh ponies are known for their friendly temperament and energy.

**Size:**
- **Section A:** Up to 12 hands (48 inches)
- **Section B:** Up to 13.2 hands (54 inches)
- **Section C:** Cob type, up to 13.2 hands (54 inches)
- **Section D:** Welsh Cob, exceeding 13.2 hands (54 inches)

**Uses:** Suitable for both children and adults, they excel in riding, driving, jumping, dressage, and showing.

## Connemara Pony

**Origin:** Ireland

**Characteristics:** Connemaras are known for their athleticism, versatility, and gentle nature. They are strong, sure-footed ponies with a refined yet sturdy build, making them capable of tackling both rugged terrain and competitive disciplines. Their even temperaments make them wonderful for riders of all ages.

**Size:** Stand between 13 to 15 hands (52 to 60 inches).

**Uses:** They excel in show jumping, dressage, eventing, endurance riding, and as reliable family ponies. Their stamina and agility make them ideal for competitive and leisure riding.

## British Riding Pony

**Origin:** United Kingdom

**Characteristics:** The British Riding Pony is a refined and elegant breed developed by crossing native British pony breeds, such as the Welsh and Dartmoor, with Arabian and Thoroughbred bloodlines. They have a graceful, athletic build with a fine head, expressive eyes, and a well-set neck. Known for their lively yet manageable temperament, British Riding Ponies are intelligent, responsive, and well-suited for young riders. They possess smooth, flowing movement and natural jumping ability, making them highly versatile.

**Size:** Typically stand between 12.2 to 14.2 hands (50 to 58 inches) at the withers.

**Uses:** British Riding Ponies are widely used in show riding, dressage, show jumping, and pony club activities. They are popular in the show ring for their beauty and performance, making them ideal for children and small adult riders in competitive and recreational riding.

## Icelandic Horse (Often Called a Pony Due to Size)

**Origin:** Iceland

**Characteristics:** Though technically a small horse, the Icelandic is often referred to as a pony due to its size. It is known for its strength, hardiness, and ability to thrive in extreme conditions. Icelandics are famous for their unique gaits, including the tölt (a smooth four-beat gait) and the pace (a two-beat lateral gait). They have a thick double coat for insulation and a strong, compact build.

**Size:** Stand between 13 to 14 hands (52 to 56 inches).

**Uses:** Icelandics are used for riding, especially in rough terrain, as well as competitive sports featuring their unique gaits. They are also treasured as versatile and trustworthy companions.

# Lesser-known Horse and Pony Breeds

## Gypsy Vanner Horse

**Origin:** United Kingdom (developed by the Romani people)

**Characteristics:** The Gypsy Vanner is a strikingly beautiful horse known for its luxurious, flowing mane and tail, as well as its signature feathering on the lower legs. They have a strong, compact build with a broad chest, powerful hindquarters, and a kind, expressive eye. Known for their calm and gentle nature, Gypsy Vanners are intelligent, willing, and friendly, making them excellent companions for riders of all levels.

**Size:** Typically stand between 13.2 to 16 hands (54 to 64 inches) at the withers.

**Uses:** Originally bred to pull Romani caravans, today they are used for driving, dressage, trail riding, and as therapy horses due to their gentle temperament. They are also popular in the show ring for their unique appearance and graceful movement.

## Akhal-Teke Horse

**Origin:** Turkmenistan

**Characteristics:** The Akhal-Teke is one of the oldest and most unique horse breeds in the world, known for its sleek, metallic coat that gives it a shimmering appearance. They are often called "The Golden Horse". This breed is slender and athletic, with a long, narrow head, fine bone structure, and a deep chest. They are renowned for their endurance, intelligence, and loyalty, often forming strong bonds with their riders. Akhal-Tekes are highly adaptable and capable of thriving in extreme climates, particularly desert conditions.

**Size:** Typically stand between 14.2 to 16 hands (58 to 64 inches) at the withers.

**Uses:** Akhal-Tekes excel in endurance riding, dressage, eventing, and show jumping. They are also valued for their stamina and speed, making them ideal for long-distance travel and competitive sports.

## Andalusian Horse (Pure Spanish Horse)

**Origin:** Spain (Andalusia region)

**Characteristics:** The Andalusian horse, also known as the Pure Spanish Horse (Pura Raza Española or PRE), is renowned for its elegance, strength, and intelligence. It has a well-proportioned, muscular build with a broad chest, strong hindquarters, and a long, flowing mane and tail. Andalusians are known for their natural collection, agility, and graceful movements, making them highly sought after for classical dressage. They have a noble and willing temperament, forming strong bonds with their handlers.

**Size:** Typically stand between 15.2 to 16.2 hands (62 to 66 inches) at the withers.

**Uses:** Andalusians excel in classical dressage, show jumping, and working equitation. They are also used for bullfighting, driving, and as parade and exhibition horses due to their impressive presence and responsiveness.

## Fjord Pony (Norwegian Fjord Horse)

**Origin:** Norway

**Characteristics:** The Fjord pony, also known as the Norwegian Fjord Horse, is one of the world's oldest and purest horse breeds, dating back over 4,000 years. It is easily recognizable by its distinctive dun-colored coat, a mane that stands upright with a dark stripe down their center, and a compact, sturdy build. Fjords are known for their gentle temperament, strength, and sure-footedness, making them ideal for work in rough terrain. Despite their stocky appearance, they are agile and versatile.

**Size:** Typically stand between 13.2 to 15 hands (54 to 60 inches) at the withers.

**Uses:** Fjords are commonly used for farm work, driving, riding, and therapeutic programs. Their calm nature and willingness to work make them suitable for riders of all levels, including children and beginners. They excel in dressage, trail riding, and working equitation.

## Fell Pony

**Origin:** England (Fell region of northern England, particularly Cumbria)

**Characteristics:** The Fell Pony is a hardy and versatile breed known for its strength, agility, and friendly temperament. It has a sturdy, compact build with a well-muscled neck, strong legs, and feathered fetlocks. Fell Ponies typically have a thick, flowing mane and tail, and they are almost always black, though brown, bay, and gray are also recognized colors. Their calm and intelligent nature makes them excellent for various equestrian activities.

**Size:** Typically stand between 13 to 14 hands (52 to 56 inches) at the withers.

**Uses:** Traditionally used for farm work, pack carrying, and riding across rough terrain, Fell Ponies today excel in driving, trekking, dressage, and as family riding ponies. Their sure-footedness and endurance make them ideal for long-distance riding and trail work.

## Chincoteague Pony

**Origin:** United States (Chincoteague and Assateague Islands, Virginia and Maryland)

**Characteristics:** The Chincoteague Pony, also known as the Assateague Pony, is a hardy and resilient breed that has adapted to the harsh conditions of the barrier islands where it originates. These ponies are known for their compact, stocky build, short legs, and

thick coats, which help them survive in the wild. They come in a variety of colors, with pinto being the most common. Despite their small size, they are strong, intelligent, and have a friendly temperament when domesticated.

**Size:** Typically stand between 12 to 14 hands (48 to 56 inches) at the withers. Ponies raised in the wild tend to be smaller, but with proper nutrition in captivity, they can grow larger.

**Uses**: Chincoteague Ponies are used for riding, driving, and as family companions. They are especially popular in children's riding programs due to their gentle nature and versatility. They are also famous for their annual "Pony Swim," where they are rounded up and swum across the channel for auction to control the herd size.

Whether they're common or rare, every breed has something unique to offer. Learning about different breeds can help you appreciate the diversity and beauty of horses and ponies from all around the world!

CHAPTER 6
# Most Common Riding Styles and Saddles

Horses are ridden in many different styles around the world, each with its unique purpose and techniques. Whether you want to compete, explore trails, or simply have fun, there's a riding style for everyone. The two most popular types of riding are usually referred to as English or Western riding. This is because of the type of saddle that's used. Let's look at each one more closely.

## Types of Saddles

A **Western Saddle** was initially built for cowboys working on the range. They might be in the saddle for hours at a time, so they were built for comfort as well as for work. They have a saddle horn in the front that could be used to wrap a rope around when they had to round up cattle out on the plains. They also have leather pieces called strings hanging on them that can be used to tie on their rope or supplies. Unlike English saddles, they also have an additional girth called the back girth that helps keep the saddle in place during heavy work.

An **English Saddle** was created initially for jumping when people were on fox hunts. It is much lighter and sits closer to the horse's body than a western saddle. It has more forward flaps under the rider's knees to give extra grip when going over jumps. English saddles come in several varieties specific to the style of riding. A racing saddle is based on an English saddle design but has very little structure to keep it lightweight and small to allow the horses to run as fast as possible. A dressage saddle is also based on an English saddle but is more heavily padded and has flaps that are not so forward to accommodate a dressage style of riding. A saddle seat saddle is very much like a dressage saddle but without all of the padding, which lets it sit close to the horse's shoulders.

## English and Western Riding Styles

### Western Pleasure

Western Pleasure is a relaxed and smooth riding style often seen in competitions. Riders guide their horses through slow and steady gaits, showing off the horse's calm and responsive nature. This style emphasizes comfort and harmony between the rider and horse.

### Western Trail

Western Trail riding is all about navigating obstacles, whether in competitions or on actual trails. Horses must be calm, sure-footed, and obedient as they cross bridges, open gates, and maneuver through tight spaces. It's a fun and practical style for both work and recreation.

### English – Hunt Seat

Hunt Seat is a traditional English riding style often associated with jumping and fox hunting. Riders focus on balance and elegance as they guide their horses over fences and through courses. In horse shows, you may see classes for Hunters under saddle and over fences. This non-jumping class is called on the flat, to show how well riders can communicate with their horses through their gaits. Hunt Seat riding is a favorite for equestrians who love speed and precision.

## English – Saddle Seat

Saddle Seat riding highlights the beauty and high-stepping gaits of certain horse breeds, like Saddlebreds and Morgans. Riders sit tall in the saddle and guide their horses to perform elegant movements. This style is often seen in showrings and is all about grace and style.

## Dressage

Dressage is like a dance between horse and rider. This riding style focuses on precise movements and communication, showcasing the horse's training and athleticism. The ultimate goal in dressage is to create the appearance of the horse doing all of the movements on his own without the help of his rider. Dressage competitions range from basic skills to advanced routines that look like ballet on horseback. Some classes even are done with music, which is especially impressive.

### Bareback

Riding bareback means riding without a saddle. It's a great way to build balance and a strong connection with your horse. Bareback riding is often done for fun or to improve riding skills, as it allows riders to feel every movement of the horse beneath them. One extremely fun bareback activity is riding your horse in a stream or actually letting your horse swim. It feels like they are galloping, but they are not really going that fast.

## Surprising Riding Styles

While the common riding styles are widely practiced, there are also some surprising and exciting styles around the world.

### Trick Riding

Trick riding is usually done with a western saddle and involves daring stunts performed while the horse is galloping. Riders might stand on the saddle, hang off the side, or perform flips. It's a thrilling and highly skilled discipline you will see at rodeos and other performances.

## Vaulting

Vaulting is like gymnastics on horseback. This sport uses a special piece of equipment called a surcingle instead of a saddle. It looks like a girth but with handles on either side of the front. Riders perform acrobatic moves, such as flips and handstands, while the horse moves on a lunge line in a circle. The vaulter mounts the horse while he is moving, does the routine, and dismounts while the horse is moving. It's a beautiful combination of athleticism and artistry.

## Side Saddle

Side saddle riding is a traditional style of horseback riding where the rider sits with both legs on one side of the horse, typically to the left. This is a highly modified English saddle in that it has only one stirrup for your left foot and a part above the stirrup that holds the rider's right leg, like crossing your legs in a chair. This elegant style has historical roots in the medieval period, originally designed to allow women in long skirts to ride without compromising modesty. It later evolved into a symbol of grace and poise, especially in the Victorian and Edwardian eras. It takes a lot of balance

and practice to learn this style of riding, and it can still be seen in some horse shows with riders in long skirts.

Each riding style offers something unique and special. No matter which one you choose, riding is a fantastic way to connect with horses and enjoy their incredible abilities.

## Polo

Polo is a fast-paced team sport played on horseback, usually with a modified English-type saddle. Riders use mallets to hit a ball into the opposing team's goal. Each rider changes horses at least four times during the match, as the horses gallop the entire time. Originating in ancient Persia, it's now a global sport requiring speed, precision, and incredible teamwork between horse and rider.

CHAPTER 7
# Taking Care of a Horse or Pony

Owning or caring for a horse or pony is a big responsibility but also an incredibly rewarding experience. Horses rely on us to meet their needs and keep them healthy and happy. Being around horses is also a responsibility to keep ourselves and our horses safe. Here's what you need to know about being around and taking care of these wonderful animals.

**Horses Communication with You**

Knowing a horse's **body language** is an important skill to learn. Horses primarily communicate through body language, and understanding their signals is essential for safe and effective interaction.

The first place to watch is the horse's **ear position**, where forward ears or ears moving in your direction indicate interest and pinned-back ears signal irritation or aggression.

A horse's **eyes and nostrils** also can reveal emotions, wide eyes and flared nostrils often indicate fear or excitement, while soft, relaxed features suggest contentment.

**Tail movement** is another important cue; a swishing tail can indicate annoyance, while a relaxed tail suggests calmness.

Watching a horse's **body posture**, such as a tense or stiff stance, can help you recognize discomfort or potential aggression. Being attentive to these signals allows for better communication and ensures a safe environment for both horse and handler.

Just remember, a horse can't see you when you're right behind them, so it's a good idea to keep a hand on them or talk to them so they always know you're there. It's like keeping the conversation going with your horse!

## Basic Needs

### Feeding

Horses need a balanced diet to stay healthy. Their diet mainly consists of hay, grass, and grains. Different types of hay include:

**Timothy Hay:** A popular choice because of its balanced nutrition.

**Alfalfa Hay:** High in protein and calcium, it's great for growing or active horses.

**Orchard Grass:** Soft and palatable, it's ideal for picky eaters.

Grains are also an important part of a horse's diet. Common grains include oats, barley, and corn. Some horses also benefit from pelleted or sweet feeds, which combine grains with added vitamins and minerals. Some horses, like people, love to eat, and some are picky eaters. It's very important to monitor what they eat because too much or too little can get them sick. Fresh, clean water should always be available, as horses drink a lot—up to 10 gallons a day! Treats like carrots and apples are a nice way to show love, but they should be given in moderation.

**Grooming**

Grooming is not only about keeping your horse clean but also about bonding with them. This is a time that both horses and humans look forward to, so leave plenty of time for this activity. Use a variety of brushes to care for their coat:

You start with the curry comb, moving it in circular motions over their coat. Dust and loose hair rise as the comb works it's magic, and your horse leans into the pressure, enjoying the gentle massage. The rhythmic movement feels calming for both of you, and it is a quiet moment to share before the day's activities begin.

Next, you pick up the hard brush, using long strokes to sweep away the dirt and debris the curry comb loosened. As you work along their back and sides, their coat starts to shine, catching the sunlight streaming through the barn. When you reach for the soft brush, your touch becomes lighter and more precise, gently brushing their face and other sensitive areas.

Combing their mane and tail is a soothing process, both for you and your horse. Carefully working through tangles with the mane comb, you notice how they seem to relax under your care. As you move to their tail, you stand off to the side for safety, making sure they're comfortable as you smooth out the long strands.

Finally, it's time for their hooves. You crouch down and gently lift one leg, holding it securely as you use the hoof pick to clean out dirt, rocks, and debris. "Good job," you murmur as your horse shifts slightly but stands still, trusting you completely. You carefully clean around the frog—the soft, triangular part in the center of the hoof—ensuring everything is spotless.

Grooming isn't just about looking good—it's essential for your horse's health. It helps you spot any cuts, swelling, or skin issues

early, and regular hoof care keeps them comfortable and ready for action. A farrier will need to trim their hooves every 6 to 8 weeks, much like trimming fingernails, but on a much larger scale.

**Exercise**

Horses need daily exercise to stay fit and happy. Most horses look forward to being turned out in a paddock each day. Some will run around, and some will just relax and enjoy the outdoors. But they also need some structured exercise, which can include riding, which is the most fun for both of you or lunging, which is exercising on a long line that resembles a long dog leash. This is an important skill you will want to learn as part of your riding lesson program, even though it's not really riding. Lunging comes in handy when you don't have time to ride, or it's too wet or snowy to turn your horse out for some exercise. A combination of activities helps maintain a horse's physical and mental health and prevents boredom.

## Shelter

Horses need a safe and comfortable place to live. A sturdy stable, or well-fenced pasture with access to shade and shelter from the elements is essential. Make sure their living area is clean and free of hazards. If your horse lives in a stall, it must be cleaned at least once per day. Stall cleaning is a great way to help out at the riding stable.

## Veterinary Care

Regular check-ups with a veterinarian are important to keep your horse healthy. They need vaccinations, deworming, and dental care. If your horse shows signs of illness, such as sluggishness or loss of appetite, contact a vet immediately.

## Emotional Well Being

Horses are social animals and thrive on interaction. Spend time with your horse daily, whether it's riding, grooming, or simply talking to them. Horses that feel loved and secure are happier and healthier.

## Safety Tips

Wear sturdy boots and a helmet when working around horses.

Always approach a horse calmly and speak softly to avoid startling them.

Learn how to safely interact with your horse by watching their body language so that you will recognize any signs of discomfort or stress.

Taking care of a horse or pony requires time, effort, and dedication, but the bond you'll form with them is worth every moment. With proper care, your horse will be a happy and healthy companion for years to come.

CHAPTER 8

# Getting Ready for Riding Lessons

Taking your first riding lesson is an exciting adventure, but properly preparing is key to making the experience safe, comfortable, and fun. Here's what you need to know before you hop in the saddle!

## Get the Right Clothing

Wearing the correct clothing for riding is essential for safety and comfort. Choose snug but not restrictive pants, like breeches, jodhpurs, or leggings. Avoid slippery materials or jeans with thick seams that could rub against your skin while riding.

For tops, wear a comfortable, close-fitting shirt that allows you to move freely. On colder days, layer with a lightweight jacket or vest that won't interfere with your posture.

## Get the Proper Boots and Helmet

Choosing the proper boots and helmet is an essential part of being prepared to ride. Your safety highly depends on these two items, in the barn and on the horse.

**Riding Boots:** Choose boots with a small heel (about 1 inch) to prevent your foot from slipping through the stirrup. Paddock boots, well-fitting cowboy boots, or tall riding boots are great choices for beginners.

**Helmet:** Always wear an ASTM/SEI-certified riding helmet. This ensures it meets safety standards and will protect your head in case of a fall. Your helmet should fit snugly without being uncomfortable and should always have a chin strap.

Never ride without proper footwear and a helmet—your safety comes first!

## Find the Right Stable and Instructor

The right environment makes all the difference in your riding experience. Look for a stable with:

- Clean and well-maintained facilities
- Calm, well-cared-for horses
- Friendly and knowledgeable staff

Your instructor should be patient, experienced, and able to explain concepts clearly. Many instructors offer a trial lesson, which is a great way to see if the stable and teaching style are a good fit for you. You can also visit a stable on lesson days and observe how the instructor teaches and how many students are in each class. Ask the instructor for referrals of current students and give them a call. It could also be a way to find friends to have lessons with.

## Review Your Horse Knowledge

Before your first riding lesson, it's important to go over what you have learned so far. Know the basic horse grooming, including the names of the brushes and tools used that you learned in Chapter 7. Remind yourself of how to keep safe at the barn, like don't walk too close behind the horses, and not to startle the horses.

Understanding basic horse behavior and body language can help you interact confidently and respectfully with the horse, like watching the horse's ears to see if he is happy with you and listening, or if he has his ears back and wants to be left alone.

Review the common riding terms in Chapter 4, like Walk on, Whoa, Trot, and the parts of the saddle and bridle. This will make it easier to follow your instructor's guidance. Finally, practice a positive and patient mindset, as riding requires both physical coordination and communication with your horse.

## Final Tips for Your First Lesson

Arrive early to meet your instructor and the horse you'll be riding. If you arrive early enough, you may be allowed to help groom and/or tack up your horse. Even if you just get to watch, you will learn how this is done.

- Don't be afraid to ask questions—everyone starts as a beginner!
- Watch everyone else at the barn to get a sense of how to behave.

- Be calm and confident around the horse; they can sense your emotions.

Be happy with each step of your progress. The more times you do the basics; the sooner you will gain confidence and be ready to learn a new skill.

Remember, the goal is to have fun and enjoy building a connection with your horse.

With the proper preparation, your first riding lesson will be a wonderful experience, marking the start of your journey into the world of horseback riding!

CHAPTER 9

# Tacking Up Your Horse or Pony

Tacking up your horse or pony is a vital skill to learn. It's important to know the proper steps to keep both you and your horse comfortable and safe. In this chapter, we'll learn how to put on both an English and a Western saddle, as well as how to fit a bridle properly. One of the key points to remember is to be sure your horse or pony knows what you are doing and where you are at all times. I like to talk to my horse and tell him what I'm up to. Even if he doesn't know every word, he hears my voice and knows where I am, especially as you walk from one side to the other side of him, leaving a wide berth when walking behind him.

## What You Need to Tack Up

Before you start, gather your tack. For English riding, you'll need an English saddle with a girth and stirrups attached, a saddle pad, and a bridle. For Western riding, you'll need a Western saddle that may or may not have two girths, a saddle blanket, and a bridle. Each type of tack is designed differently, so let's look at how to use them!

## English Saddles

An English saddle is lightweight and sleek, and as we discussed earlier, it is designed for activities like jumping, dressage, or casual riding. It has a pommel (the raised part at the front), a seat, a cantle in the back, and stirrups attached by stirrup leathers. Let's go through how to tack up the English horse.

Start with a well-groomed horse or pony that is tied or cross-tied in the grooming area. The first piece of equipment you will use is the Saddle Pad. Be sure the underside that goes against the horse is soft and free of anything that might irritate him. You may have to give it a quick brush. Place the saddle pad just above your horse's withers, (the high point between its shoulders). Then you can slide it back into place on your horse's back, just behind its withers. This ensures the horse's hair is flat, also avoiding anything that might cause him discomfort. Make sure the pad is evenly placed and lifted up a little bit in the center so that it doesn't get tight when the saddle is on top of it. Be sure to have your instructor check each time you do this until you are confident of its placement.

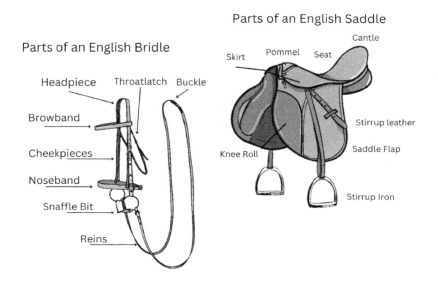

Then, prepare to put on the saddle. Hold the saddle with your left hand under the front, or pommel, and your right hand under the back, or cantle. Be sure the stirrups are run up on the leathers neatly, and if the girth is attached, have it folded over the top of the saddle towards you. Lift the saddle and gently place it on top of the saddle pad. Adjust it so it's centered, and the pommel is just behind the horse's withers. Again, have your instructor check all of your work. Then you are ready to fasten the girth. If the girth is already attached on the saddle's far side or right side, you will walk around the horse and take it down gently. If not, you will fasten it to the right side first. Then, walk back to the near side, the left of the horse, and secure it snugly. The girth should be tight enough to keep the saddle in place but not so tight that it makes your horse uncomfortable. You will give it another tightening just before you mount because most horses relax after a few minutes of feeling the saddle on their backs.

## Western Saddles

A Western saddle is larger, heavier and built for long rides and activities like trail riding or barrel racing. It has a horn, like a knob, on top of the pommel at the front, a deep seat, a skirt all around, and wide fenders that hold the stirrups. Now, let's go through putting it on your horse.

Again, you will start with a well-groomed horse or pony that is tied or cross-tied in the grooming area. And again, the first piece of your tack is the Saddle Blanket. This is usually different from a saddle pad, as it is actually a blanket that is traditionally used to go under the saddle. Still, now there are saddle pads that are specifically made for western saddles for people who prefer them. Whichever you use, you will be sure it is comfortable and well placed on your horse's back, making sure it's smooth and even.

To put this saddle on, you will lift the Western saddle (you might need a little muscle for this!) and place it gently on the saddle blanket. Just like the English saddle, be sure nothing is hanging on the right side of the saddle. Fold the right stirrup and any attached

Parts of the Western Bridle

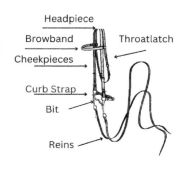

Parts of the Western Saddle

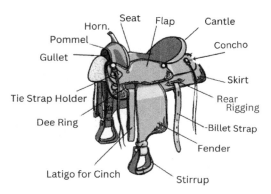

girths over the top of the saddle so when you gently place it on the horse, nothing is slapping or startling the horse on the far side. The saddle's horn should be over the horse's withers. Walk around to the off side of the horse and let down the stirrup and girth. On a western saddle, the girth, or cinch, which is another name for a western girth, is usually attached to the right side already. It can be a string cinch, made from cotton, wool, or mohair, or a leather cinch. If there is a back cinch, it is commonly made of leather. Tightening the cinch on a western saddle is slightly more complicated than an English saddle. Still, with practice, you will find it easy. So, go back to the horse's left side and unfold the latigo, the long strap, from its keeper. You will now reach under the horse's belly and grab the cinch. It will have a ring on the end, which you will loop the latigo through, then up to the saddle ring, and back through the cinch again, which will allow you to tighten it securely but comfortably. This takes a little practice to perfect, so be sure you have help the first few times. If there is a back cinch, you will need to be very sure that it is not too tight or too loose. This is something someone more experienced should do for you to prevent discomfort for the horse.

## The Bridle

The purpose of the bridle is to allow you to guide, or steer, your horse during the ride. There are some differences in bridles for Western or English riding, and some things are the same. They always include a headpiece, which includes the throatlatch, a bit (which goes in the horse's mouth), and reins. English bridles also have a noseband and a browband; some Western bridles may have one or the other also included. The biggest difference is in the bit. A western bit is usually designed for the rider to "neck rein" the horse, usually on a very loose contact with the horse's mouth. In contrast, an English bit is designed for a more direct feel of the horse's mouth with a shorter rein. Whichever you use, let's see how to put it on your horse.

Start by untying your horse from the cross ties or post. Stand on his left side and place the lead rope over your horse's neck. Always be sure the lead rope or halter is not in a position to get you or the horse tangled up. You will then unbuckle the halter and re-buckle it around his neck. This is to ensure that your horse doesn't decide to wander away from you. Some instructors may teach you to put the reins from the bridle over the horse's head so you don't have to use the halter and lead rope. You should always ask which way they prefer because some horses are used to a specific routine. You are then ready to hold the top of the bridle with your right hand and let the bit rest in your left palm. Lift the bridle with the reins up towards the horse's ears while you guide the bit into the horse's mouth. Once the horse has the bit in his mouth, you continue to lift the bridle and start by placing the horse's right ear under the headpiece and then the left, ensuring nothing is pinched. Some western bridles only have a place for the right ear to go through. Let the reins go down his neck, and you can remove the halter and lead line, as you now have the bridle and reins to keep him with you. Next, fasten the throatlatch, (the strap that goes under the horse's throat) leaving plenty of slack, about three finger's width. And lastly, tighten the noseband if there is one, so it is snug.

## Final Checks

Before you ride, double-check everything! Make sure the saddle and bridle are secure and that your horse looks comfortable. Adjust anything that seems off to prevent discomfort during the ride.

Tacking up your horse or pony can take a little practice, but it will become second nature with time. Always remember to work calmly and gently, showing your horse that they're in good hands. Now you're ready to ride and enjoy your time together!

CHAPTER 10
# Let's Begin Riding!

## Your First Lesson

The moment has arrived—you're finally about to ride! You are taking your first group riding lesson. As you approach your assigned horse, excitement bubbles in your chest. You are riding Joey today. He is a beautiful bay horse with a black mane and tail. Lisa, the helper at the stable, tells you that he is 14.2 hands tall, so he is actually considered a pony. He sure looks like a horse, though! The sunlight glints off Joey's well-groomed coat, and he stands patiently, ears flicking as he listens to the gentle sounds of the stable. You lead Joey to the mounting block, and with a deep breath, you remind yourself of everything you've learned so far.

### Mounting

Mounting the horse feels like the first step into a new world. You start by checking the saddle and girth, ensuring everything is secure. Joey looks around slightly, sensing your presence, but stays calm as you step up onto the mounting block.

"Hold the reins in your left hand," your instructor reminds you. You grip the front of the saddle, placing your left foot into the stirrup. With a steady push, you swing your right leg over the horse's

back. For a brief moment, you hover, feeling the thrill of being up high, before settling gently into the saddle.

Joey shifts beneath you, his body warm and strong. You let out a small laugh—you're really riding!

**Settling into the Saddle**

Sitting in the saddle feels a bit wobbly at first, but you straighten your back and take a deep breath. "Relax your shoulders," the instructor says, and you let the tension melt away. Your feet find the stirrups, and your instructor adjusts them until they feel even. You will learn how to do this yourself before long.

As the horse stands still, you take a moment to notice how your body connects with his. You feel the steady rise and fall of his breathing and begin to relax. With your hands low and steady on the reins, you're ready to begin.

**Walk On**

"Ask your horses to walk on," your instructor tells everyone. You lightly squeeze your calves against Joey's sides and say, "Walk on," in a clear, calm voice. He responds immediately, stepping forward with a gentle rhythm.

At first, the movement feels strange, like trying to balance on a moving wave. But soon, you find yourself swaying naturally with the horse's stride. The sound of hooves on the ground creates a calming rhythm, and a smile spreads across your face.

## The Reins: A Language of Touch

The reins are your connection to the horse's head, a way to guide them with small, gentle movements. "Think of the reins as a conversation," your instructor says. You hold them lightly, as if cradling something fragile, keeping your hands even and steady.

As the horse moves, you experiment with small tugs and releases, learning how a simple touch can communicate so much. Joey flicks his ears back at you, responding to your cues. It feels like magic—the two of you working together as a team.

### Heels Down

"Heels down!" the instructor calls out. You adjust your position, lowering your heels until they're angled downward. At first, it feels awkward, but then you realize how much steadier it makes you. Your legs hug the horse's sides gently, and you feel more balanced.

Lowering your heels keeps your body aligned, making you feel secure even as the horse steps over uneven ground. You remind yourself to relax your toes and let your legs drape naturally.

### The Half Seat

As the lesson progresses, your instructor introduces the half seat. You lift yourself slightly out of the saddle, bending your knees and balancing over the stirrups. It's harder than it looks—your legs ache, and you wobble a bit at first.

But then you feel it: the freedom of moving with the horse, not just sitting on them. In the half seat, you're light and connected, letting the horse move more freely. You feel like you're flying, even though you're just walking.

## Finding Balance

Balance isn't about sitting stiffly; it's about moving with the horse. "Imagine a straight line from your head to your heels," your instructor says. You focus on staying centered, letting your hips sway gently with the horse's stride.

As you relax, you notice how much easier it is to stay steady. Joey seems to sense your growing confidence, and his steps are becoming smoother. Riding starts to feel less like a challenge and more like a dance.

## The Dismount

All too soon, the lesson is over. Joey comes to a halt as you gently pull back on the reins and say, "Whoa." You remove your feet from the stirrups, feeling slightly reluctant to leave the saddle.

"Swing your leg over and slide down," your instructor says. You lean forward slightly, swinging your right leg over the horse's back, and hop gently to the ground. As your feet touch the earth, you feel a sense of pride—you've done it!

You pat Joey's neck, murmuring softly, "Thank you." He lowers his head slightly, as if acknowledging your gratitude. It feels like you have a new best friend!

**You Did It!**

Your first ride is a moment you'll always remember. From mounting to dismounting, every step taught you something new—not just about horses, but about yourself. Riding is a partnership, a blend of trust, communication, and practice.

As you lead Joey back to the stable, you can't help but feel excited for your next lesson. This is just the beginning of your journey as an equestrian!

CHAPTER 11

# Continue Your Riding Adventures

Riding lessons once a week at your local stable are a great way to build your riding and horsemanship skills. However, once you develop your confidence and have a good grasp of the basics, you may want to consider other riding and learning opportunities that are available.

## Horse Camps and Competitions: Summer Fun and Challenges

Whether you're a beginner or an experienced rider, horse camps and competitions offer a blend of fun, learning, and challenge that makes every day feel like an adventure.

### The Magic of Horse Camps

Imagine spending your summer days surrounded by horses, making new friends, and learning something new every day. Horse camps are an immersive equestrian experience, a place where horse lovers come together to grow their skills and have fun.

From the moment you arrive, the camp is alive with activity. Horses are being groomed, riders are practicing in the arenas, and the air is filled with the soft nickering of horses and the laughter of new friends. The counselors greet you warmly, introducing you to your horse for the week—a gentle and curious bay mare named Bella.

**Riding Lessons and Skill-Building**

Each morning starts with riding lessons tailored to your level. For beginners, the focus might be on mastering the basics: steering, stopping, and keeping your heels down. For more advanced riders, it's all about refining skills like jumping or trail riding.

Bella is patient as you practice posting at the trot. Your instructor offers gentle corrections, and soon, you're moving in rhythm with Bella's steps. The thrill of improvement—of getting something just right—makes you beam with pride.

But horse camp isn't just about riding. In the afternoons, you dive into hands-on workshops where you learn to care for the horses.

Grooming, feeding, mucking stalls—it's all part of the experience. As you brush Bella's shiny coat, you feel the connection between you growing stronger.

**Friendships and Growth**

One of the best parts of horse camp is the friendships you make. Sharing your love of horses with others creates bonds that can last a lifetime. During lunch breaks, you and your new friends swap stories about your favorite horses and cheer each other on during lessons.

Horse camp also teaches independence and responsibility. Every camper has chores to complete—filling water buckets, sweeping the barn aisle, or cleaning tack. It might seem like hard work at first. Still, soon, you realize how satisfying it feels to contribute to caring for these amazing animals.

**The Competitive Side: Horse Shows**

For some, horse camp is just the beginning. The competitive world

of equestrian activities opens up a new realm of challenges and achievements.

Your instructor mentions a local horse show happening at the end of camp, and suddenly, the lessons take on a new level of excitement. You'll get to compete! The idea of riding Bella in front of judges and an audience is both thrilling and a little nerve-wracking.

**Local and Regional Horse Shows**

At the horse show, the atmosphere is electric. Riders in polished boots and freshly brushed horses fill the grounds. The air smells of leather, hay, and just a hint of nervous energy.

Your event is a simple walk-trot class, perfect for beginners. Your heart races as you enter the arena, but Bella's calm demeanor steadies you. The judge watches closely as you guide her around the arena. You focus on everything you've learned; heels down, hands steady, and shoulders back.

When the results are announced, you're overjoyed to receive a ribbon. It's not just about winning; it's about knowing you gave it your best.

For more experienced riders, regional shows offer the chance to compete in jumping, dressage, barrel racing, or even team events like relay races. Each competition is a chance to showcase your skills and learn from others.

## The Joy of Challenges

Whether you're at camp or competing in a show, every moment is an opportunity to grow. You learn to face challenges with determination, celebrate small victories, and support your friends along the way.

Horse camps and competitions remind us that the journey with horses is about more than just riding—it's about adventure, connection, and discovering what you're capable of.

## Conclusion: A New World Awaits

As we come to the end of this book, it's clear that the world of horses and ponies is as magical as it is diverse. From their gentle and loving nature to their incredible strength and versatility, these majestic creatures have captured our hearts and inspired countless adventures.

You've explored why we love horses, learned about their many jobs, discovered different breeds, and imagined yourself mastering riding styles or caring for a horse of your own. Whether you dream of spending summers at horse camp, entering your first competition, or simply enjoying the beauty of horses from afar, there's a place for everyone in the equestrian world.

Horses teach us lessons that go beyond the barn or the saddle. They show us the value of patience, trust, and hard work. They encourage us to connect with nature and to approach life with curiosity and courage. Through every moment spent with a horse—whether grooming, riding, or simply watching them graze—we grow in ways we never expected.

Now, it's your turn to take the reins. Whether you're heading to your first lesson, signing up for horse camp, or just dreaming of riding one day, the journey ahead is full of excitement and possibility. Horses and ponies are waiting to share their world with you—a world of adventure, friendship, and joy.

So, saddle up and enjoy the ride. The journey is just beginning!

Printed in Great Britain
by Amazon